INTERNET:
AN OVERVIEW OF KEY TECHNOLOGY POLICY ISSUES AFFECTING ITS USE AND GROWTH

INTERNET:
AN OVERVIEW OF KEY TECHNOLOGY POLICY ISSUES AFFECTING ITS USE AND GROWTH

MARCIA S. SMITH, JOHN D. MOTEFF,
LENNARD G. KRUGER, GLENN J. MCLOUGHLIN
AND JEFFREY W. SEIFERT

Novinka Books
New York

Senior Editors: Susan Boriotti and Donna Dennis
Coordinating Editor: Tatiana Shohov
Office Manager: Annette Hellinger
Graphics: Wanda Serrano
Editorial Production: Jennifer Vogt, Matthew Kozlowski and Maya Columbus
Circulation: Ave Maria Gonzalez, Indah Becker, Raymond Davis and Vladimir Klestov
Communications and Acquisitions: Serge P. Shohov
Marketing: Cathy DeGregory

Library of Congress Cataloging-in-Publication Data
Available Upon Request

ISBN 1-59033-285-7

Copyright © 2002 by Nova Science Publishers, Inc.
400 Oser Ave, Suite 1600
Hauppauge, New York 11788-3619
Tele. 631-231-7269   Fax 631-231-8175
e-mail: Novascience@earthlink.net
Web Site: http://www.novapublishers.com

All rights reserved. No part of this book may be reproduced, stored in a retrieval system or transmitted in any form or by any means: electronic, electrostatic, magnetic, tape, mechanical photocopying, recording or otherwise without permission from the publishers.

The publisher has taken reasonable care in the preparation of this book, but makes no expressed or implied warranty of any kind and assumes no responsibility for any errors or omissions. No liability is assumed for incidental or consequential damages in connection with or arising out of information contained in this book.

This publication is designed to provide accurate and authoritative information with regard to the subject matter covered herein. It is sold with the clear understanding that the publisher is not engaged in rendering legal or any other professional services. If legal or any other expert assistance is required, the services of a competent person should be sought. FROM A DECLARATION OF PARTICIPANTS JOINTLY ADOPTED BY A COMMITTEE OF THE AMERICAN BAR ASSOCIATION AND A COMMITTEE OF PUBLISHERS.

Printed in the United States of America

CONTENTS

Preface	vii
Internet Privacy	1
Computer Security	9
Broadband Internet Access	14
Electronic Commerce	19
Unsolicited Commercial Electronic Mail ("Junk E-Mail" or "Spam")	25
Internet Domain Names	27
Government Information Technology Management	32
Appendix A: Legislation in the 107th Congress	39
Appendix B: List of Acronyms	44
Appendix C: Legislation Passed by the 105th and 106th Congresses	47
Index	53

PREFACE

This book presents an overview of the following key technology policy areas: internet privacy; concerns about computer security; broadband internet access; electronic commerce (e-commerce); unsolicited commercial electronic mail (UCE), or "junk e-mail" or "spam"; how the administration and governance of the internet's domain name system (DNS) is currently under transition from federal to private sector control; three major themes characterize legislative activity and interest: internet infrastructure development, resource management, and the provision of online services by the government (called "e-government").

INTERNET: AN OVERVIEW OF KEY TECHNOLOGY POLICY ISSUES AFFECTING ITS USE AND GROWTH

INTERNET PRIVACY[1]

Internet privacy issues encompass a range of concerns. One is that the Internet makes it easier for governmental and private sector entities to obtain information about consumers and possibly use that information to the consumers' detriment. That issue focuses on the extent to which Web site operators collect personally identifiable information about individuals and share that information with third parties, often without the knowledge or consent of the people concerned.

Another aspect of Internet privacy is the extent to which Internet activities such as electronic mail (e-mail) and visits to Web sites are monitored by law enforcement officials or employers. In the wake of the September 11 terrorist attacks, the issue of law enforcement monitoring of Internet activity has become more controversial, with some advocating additional tools for law enforcement to fight terrorism, and others cautioning that basic tenets of our democracy, such as privacy, not be sacrificed in the effort.

---

[1] CRS Report RS20035, *Internet Privacy – Protecting Personal Information: Overview and Pending Legislation*, by Marcia S. Smith, provides an overview of Internet privacy issues and tracks pending legislation. It is updated more frequently than this report. CRS Report RL30784, *Internet Privacy: An Analysis of Technology and Policy Issues*, by Marcia S. Smith, provides more comprehensive analysis of many of the issues involved in this debate.

Although not an Internet privacy issue per se, consumer identity theft often arises in the Internet privacy context because of the perception that Social Security numbers and credit card numbers are more readily accessible because of the Internet.

More than 30 bills in the 106th Congress addressed Internet privacy issues in whole or in part.[2] The only legislation that cleared Congress and was signed into law, however, were amendments to the FY2001 Transportation Appropriations Act (P.L. 106-346) and the FY2001 Transportation Appropriations Act (including the Consolidated Appropriations Act, P.L. 106-554) addressing the use of "cookies" on certain federal agency Web sites. The 107th Congress continues to have a strong interest in Internet privacy issues. Medical records privacy and financial records privacy are not Internet privacy issues.

Collection of Data by Web Site Operators and Fair Information Practices

Perhaps the most often discussed Internet privacy issue is whether commercial Web sites should be required to adhere to four "fair information practices" proposed by the Federal Trade Commission (FTC): providing *notice* to users of their information practices before collecting personal information, allowing users *access* to data collected and the ability to contest its accuracy, and ensuring *security* of the information from unauthorized use. In particular, the question is whether industry can be relied upon to regulate itself, or if legislation is needed to protect consumer privacy. Questions also have arisen about whether federal government Web sites should have to adhere to such practices.

Commercial Web Sites

The FTC has been very active on Internet privacy issues for several years. Based on a series of surveys of commercial Web sites each year since 1997, the FTC has issued reports and made recommendations about whether legislation is needed to protect consumer privacy on the Web. Although the FTC and the Clinton Administration favored self regulation, in 1998, frustrated at industry's slow pace, the FTC announced that it would seek

---

[2] For a list of the 106th Congress Internet privacy bills, see Appendix B of CRS Report RL30784, *Internet Privacy: An Analysis of Technology and Policy Issues.*

legislation protecting children's privacy on the Internet by requiring parental permission before a Web site could request information about a child under 13. The Children's Online Privacy Protection Act (COPPA, part of P.L. 105-277) was enacted four months later.

In 1999, the FTC concluded that further legislation was not needed at that time for children or adults, but reversed its decision in 2000 when another survey indicated that industry still was not self regulating to the desired extent. The FTC voted 3-2 to propose legislation that would allow it to establish regulations requiring Web site operators to follow the four fair information practices. The close vote underscored the controversial nature of the FTC's reversal of position, which was further illuminated at a Senate Commerce Committee hearing on May 25, 2000.

In June 2001, Timothy Muris replaced Robert Pitofsky as FTC chairman. On October 4, 2001, Mr. Muris gave a speech revealing his position on the issue. He does not see a need for additional legislation now, preferring strong enforcement of existing regulations coupled with industry self-regulation instead.

The Internet industry has taken steps to demonstrate that it can self regulate. One example is the formation of the Online Privacy Alliance (OPA), a group of more than 80 companies and associations in the Internet business. OPA developed a set of privacy guidelines and its members are required to adopt a privacy policy, post it on their site(s), and implement the policy. Another is the establishment of "seals" for Web sites by the Better Business Bureau, TRUSTe, and WebTrust. To display a seal from one of those organizations, a Web site operator must agree to abide by certain privacy principles (some of which are based on the OPA guidelines), a complaint resolution process, and to being monitored for compliance. Advocates of self regulation argue that these seal programs demonstrate industry's ability to police itself. Advocates of further legislation argue that while the seal programs are useful, they do not carry the weight of law, limiting remedies for consumers whose privacy has been violated. They also point out the while a site may disclose its privacy policy, that does not necessarily equate to having a policy that protects privacy.

Federal Web Sites

Until the summer of 2000, attention was focused on privacy issues associated with commercial Web sites. That changed in June 2000, however, when controversy erupted over the privacy of visitors to government Web sites. Dubbed "Cookiegate" in the press, the issue concerned federal agencies' use of computer "cookies" (small text files placed on users' computers when they access a particular Web site) to track activity at their Web sites. Federal agencies had been directed by President Clinton and the Office of Management and Budget (OMB) to ensure that their information collection practices adhere to the Privacy Act of 1974. A September 5, 2000 letter from OMB to the Department of Commerce further clarified that "persistent" cookies, which remain on a user's computer for varying lengths of time (from hours to years), are not allowed unless four specific conditions are met. "Session" cookies, which expire when the user exits the browser, are permitted.

In June 2000, however, the Clinton White House announced that it had just learned that contractors for the Office of National Drug Control Policy (ONDCP) had been using cookies to collect information about those using ONDCP's Web site during an anti-drug campaign wherein users clicking on anti-drug ads on various Web sites were taken to an ONDCP site. Cookies then were placed on users' computers to count the number of users, what ads they clicked on, and what pages they viewed on the ONDCP site. The White House directed ONDCP to cease using cookies, and OMB issued a memorandum reminding agencies to post and comply with privacy policies and detailing the limited circumstances under which agencies should collect personal information.

Congress reacted to the overall concern about federal agency information practices on Web sites by adding language concerning such activities by departments and agencies funded in the FY2001 Treasury-General Government Appropriations Act, commonly called the "Treasury-Postal Act." The language is contained both in the FY2001 Treasury-Postal Appropriations Act itself, and in the FY2001 Transportation Appropriations Act. Section 501 of the FY2001 Transportation Appropriations Act (P.L. 106-346) prohibits funds in the FY2001 Treasury-Postal act from being used by any federal agency to collect, review, or create aggregate lists that include personally identifiable information (PII) about an individual's access to or use of a federal Web site or enter into agreements with third parties to do so, with exceptions. Section 646 of the FY2001 Treasury-Postal Act, as included in the FY2001 Consolidated Appropriations Act (P.L. 106-554), requires Inspectors General (IGs) of agencies or departments to report to Congress within 60 days of enactment on activities by those agencies or departments relating to collection of PII about individuals who access any Internet site of that department or agency, or entering into agreements with third parties to obtain PII about use of government or non-government Web sites.

Senator Thompson released two reports (on April 16, 2001 and June 15, 2001) based on the findings of agency IGs who discovered unauthorized persistent cookies and other violations of government privacy guidelines. These reports can be found online at [http://www.senate.gov/~thompson/pr061501.html] and at [http://www.senate.gov/~gov_affairs/041601a_press. htm]. An April 2001 GAO report (GAO-01-424) on implementation of federal guidance for agency use of cookies concluded that as of January 2001, 57 of the 65 sites it reviewed were following OMB's guidance. In the case of those that were not, GAO reported that the relevant agencies took corrective action or said they would after GAO brought the problem to their attention. On April 9, 2001, Representative Armey issued a statement calling for the government to review its own privacy practices before imposing new requirements on commercial Web sites.

The FY2002 Treasury-Postal Appropriations Act (P.L. 107-67) prohibits, with exceptions, federal funds from being used by a federal agency to collect, review, or create any aggregate list, derived from any means, that includes the collection of any PII related to an individual's access to or use of a federal Web site, or to enter into any agreement with a third party to collect, review, or obtain such information on use of any non-governmental Web site.

S. 851 (Thompson) would establish an 18-month commission to study the collection, use, and distribution of personal information by federal, state, and local governments. H.R. 583 (Hutchinson) would create a commission to study privacy issues more broadly. Section 218 of S. 803 (Lieberman) would set requirements on government agencies in how they assure the privacy of PII in government information systems, and establish privacy guidelines for federal Web sites.

Monitoring of E-Mail and Web Activity

Law Enforcement Monitoring

Another Internet privacy storm broke in the summer of 2000 when it became known that the FBI, with a court order, installs software on Internet Service Providers' equipment to intercept e-mail and monitor an individual's Web activity. The extent to which that software program, originally called Carnivore, can differentiate between e-mail and Web activity involving a subject of an FBI investigation and other people's e-mail and Web activity is of considerable debate, with critics claiming that Carnivore violates the privacy of innocent users. A House Judiciary subcommittee held a hearing on Carnivore on July 24, 2000. Legislation that would have, *inter alia*, required law enforcement to report on its use of e-mail intercepts was discussed at a September 6, 2000 Senate Judiciary hearing. No legislation cleared the 106th Congress, however. The FBI since has renamed the program "DCS 1000." The FY2002 Department of Justice authorization bill (H.R. 2215/S.1319) as passed by the House and reported from the Senate Judiciary Committee requires the Justice Department to report to Congress on its use of DCS 1000 or any similar system. The reports required by the House and Senate versions are somewhat different.

Following the September 11 terrorist attacks, attention focused on whether law enforcement officials required new tools to combat terrorism, including additional authority to monitor Internet activity. After several weeks of debate, Congress passed and the President signed into law the USA PATRIOT Act (P.L. 107-56) that does just that. Civil liberties groups have expressed concern about the potential ramifications of the new Act on this and other grounds. They assert that they will monitor law enforcement use of the new powers to determine if any need to be challenged in court. In summary, Title II of P.L. 107-56 —

- expands the scope of subpoenas for records of electronic communications to include records commonly associated with Internet usage, such as session times and duration (Section 210);

- *allows* ISPs to divulge records or other information (but not the contents of communications) pertaining to a subscriber if they believe there is immediate danger of death or serious physical injury or as otherwise authorized, and *requires* them to divulge such records or information (excluding contents of communications) to a governmental entity under certain conditions (Section 212);

- adds routing and addressing information (used in Internet communications) to dialing information to the information a government agency may capture using pen registers and trap and trace devices as authorized by court order, while excluding the content of any wire or electronic communications (Section 216). The section also requires law enforcement officials to keep certain records when they use their own pen registers or trap and trace devices and to provide those records to the court that issued the order within 30 days of expiration of the order. To the extent that

Carnivore-like systems fall with the new definition of pen registers or trap and trace devices provided in the Act, that language would increase judicial oversight of the use of such system; and

- allows a person acting under color of law to intercept the wire or electronic communications of a computer trespasser transmitted to, through, or from a protected computer under certain circumstances.

Section 224 sets a 4-year sunset period for many of the Title II provisions, but among the sections excluded from the sunset are Sections 210 and 216.

Privacy advocates worry that, in this emotionally charged climate, Congress is passing legislation that it later will regret. Groups such as the American Civil Liberties Union (ACLU), Center for Democracy and Technology (CDT), and Electronic Privacy Information Center (EPIC) urge caution, fearful that, in an attempt to track down and punish the terrorists who threaten American democracy, one of the fundamental tenets of that democracy – privacy – may itself by threatened. The ACLU issued a press release of October 24 stating that it was deeply disappointed with the House passage of the bill. CDT's Executive Director said on October 25 [http://www.cdt.org/press/011025press.shtml] that "This bill has been called a compromise but the only thing compromised is our civil liberties."

Employer Monitoring

An emerging issue is whether employers should be required to notify their employees if e-mail or other computer-based activities are monitored. A 2001 American Management Association survey, which is available at [http://www.amanet.org/press/amanews/ems2001.htm], found that 62.8% of the companies surveyed monitor Internet connections, 46.5% store and review e-mail, and 36.1% store and review computer files. The public policy concern appears to be less about whether companies should be able to monitor activity, but whether they should notify their employees of that monitoring.

Spyware

Some software products include, as part of the software itself, a method by which information is collected about the use of the computer on which the software is installed. When the computer is connected to the Internet, the software periodically relays the information it has collected back to the software manufacturer or a marketing company. The software that performs the collection and reporting function is called "spyware." Software programs that include spyware can be obtained on a disk or downloaded from the Internet. They may be sold or provided for free. Typically, users have no knowledge that the software product they are using includes spyware. Some argue that users should be notified if the software they are using includes spyware. Two bills (H.R.112 and S. 197) have been introduced in the 107th Congress to require such notification.

Consumer Identity Theft and Protecting Social Security Numbers

The widespread use of computers for storing and transmitting information is thought by some to be contributing to consumer identity theft, in which one individual assumes the identity of another using personal information such as credit card and Social Security numbers. Government agencies report sharply increasing numbers of consumer identity theft cases, but whether the Internet is responsible is debatable. Some attribute the rise instead to carelessness by businesses in handling personally identifiable information, and by credit issuers that grant credit without proper checks. The FTC found that less that 1% of identity theft cases are linked to the Internet (*Computerworld*, February 12, 2001, p. 7). The FTC has a toll-free number (877-ID-THEFT) to help victims of identity theft.

Although not related directly to whether Social Security numbers are more accessible because of the Internet, it should be noted that the 105th Congress passed the Identity Theft and Assumption Deterrence Act (P.L. 105-318). That Act sets penalties for persons who knowingly, and with the intent to commit unlawful activities, possess, transfer, or use one or more means of identification not legally issued for use to that person. Also, the 106th Congress passed the Social Security Number Confidentiality Act (P.L. 106-433, H.R. 3218) which prohibits the display of SSNs on unopened checks or other Treasury-issued drafts. Furthermore, the 106th Congress passed the Internet False Identification Act (P.L. 106-578), which updates existing law against selling or distributing false Ids to include those sold or distributed through computer files, templates, and disks.

Several bills have been introduced in the 107th Congress relating to identity theft or protection of Social Security numbers (H.R. 91, H.R. 220, H.R. 1478, H.R./S. 1014, S. 848, and H.R. 3053/S. 1399). In 2001, hearings have been held by House Ways and Means and House Financial Services subcommittees (November 8), and a Senate Judiciary subcommittee (September 13).

COMPUTER SECURITY

As use of the Internet grows, so has concern about security of and on the Internet. Widespread media attention to recent security-related incidents (the most recent being the Code Red and Code Red II worms, which disrupt Windows-based Internet servers) represents the tip of the iceberg. Every day, persons gain access, or try to gain access, to someone else's computer without authorization to read, copy, modify, or destroy the information contained within. These persons range from juveniles to disgruntled (ex)employees, to criminals, to competitors, to politically or socially motivated groups, to agents of foreign governments.

The extent of the problem is unknown. Not every person or company whose computer system has been compromised reports it either to the media or to authorities. Sometimes the victim judges the incident not to be worth the trouble. Sometimes the victim may judge that the adverse publicity would have been worse. Sometimes the affected parties don't even know their systems have been compromised.

There is some evidence to suggest, however, that the number of incidents is increasing. According to the Computer Emergency Response Team (CERT) at Carnegie-Mellon University, the number of incidents reported to it has grown just about every year since the team's establishment – from 132 incidents in 1989 to almost 23,000 incidents in 2000. In just the first half of 2001, over 15,000 incidents have been reported. The Computer Security Institute (CSI), in cooperation with the Federal Bureau of Investigation (FBI), has conducted an annual survey since 1996. For those responding to the question of whether they have experienced unauthorized use of their computer systems in the last 12 months, the percentage answering yes has risen from 42% in 1996 to 85% in 2001.[3]

The impact on society from the unauthorized access or use of computers is also unknown. Again, some victims may choose not to report losses. In many cases, it is difficult or impossible to quantify the losses. But social

---

[3] The CSI/FBI survey is not a scientific sampling of the nation's computer systems. Surveys are sent to computer security practitioners in U.S. corporations and

losses are not zero. Trust in one's system may be reduced. Proprietary and/or customer information (including credit card numbers) may be compromised. Any unwanted code must be found and removed. The veracity of the system's data must be checked and restored if necessary. Money may be stolen from accounts or extorted from the victim. If disruptions occur, sales may be lost. If adverse publicity occurs, future sales may be lost and stock prices may be affected. Estimate of the overall financial losses due to unauthorized access vary and their accuracy is untested. Estimates typically range in the billions of dollars per major event like the Love Bug virus or the denial-of-service attacks in February 2000. Similar estimates have been made for the Code Red worms. Estimates of losses internationally range up to the tens of billions of dollars. Those able and willing to estimate financial losses in the 2000 CSI/FBI survey estimated a total of $378 million in losses in previous 12 months.[4]

Aside from the losses discussed above, there is also growing concern that unauthorized access to computer systems could pose an overall national security risk should it result in the disruption of the nation's critical infrastructures (e.g., transportation systems, banking and finance, electric power generation and distribution). These infrastructures rely increasingly on computer networks to operate, and are themselves linked by computer and communication networks. To address this concern, President Clinton issued a Presidential Decision Directive (PDD-63) in May 1998. PDD-63 set as a national goal the ability to protect critical infrastructures from intentional attacks (both physical and cyber) by 2003. It set up organizational and operational structures within the federal government to help achieve this goal and called for a coordinated effort to engage the private sector. The Bush Administration has chosen to follow a slightly different organizational structure for coordinating that policy and its implementation.

As a deterrent, the federal computer fraud and abuse statute, 18 U.S.C. 1030, makes it a federal crime to gain unauthorized access to federal government computers, to be exposed to certain information contained on government computers, to damage to threaten to damage federal computers, bank computers, or computers used in interstate commerce, to traffic in passwords for these computers, to commit fraud from these computers, or

---

government agencies. In 2001, 538 surveys were sent out; 532 respondents answered the questions about unauthorized use.
[4] 64% of the 2001 CSI/FBI survey respondents acknowledged financial losses; 35% of them could quantify those losses. These percentages are down from the previous year, but the total estimated losses are about $100 million greater. A majority of the losses were attributed to loss of proprietary information and fraud.

from accessing a computer to commit espionage. The stature also provides for penalties. Most experts believe these statutes are sufficient to prosecute most if not all unauthorized access incidents that have occurred to date. Even so, a number of bills were introduced in the second session of the 106th Congress to increase the federal penalties associated with these crimes. None of these bills was enacted. While many experts agree that the statutes are sufficient for prosecution, many also suggest that the ability to follow the electronic trail of a hacker across jurisdictional lines is procedurally difficult. This issue was addressed in the anti-terrorism bill (P.L. 107-56) passed in the wake of the September 11 terrorist attacks.

At the international level, the 41-country Council of Europe is negotiating a treaty to facilitate tracking cyber criminals across national boundaries. The final draft of the treaty was completed in June 2001. The United States has been an observer at these negotiations. U.S. businesses have expressed some concern about their liability and the costs associated with record-keeping under this treaty. A discussion of the treaty can be found on the Council's web page, at [http://conventions.coe.int/treaty/EN/cadreprojets.htm].[5]

While the tools for prosecuting appear to be in place, most experts agree that much more can be done to make the Internet and its users more secure. The federal government is required to protect sensitive information on its own computers. The Computer Security Act of 1987 authorizes the National Institute of Standards and Technology (NIST) to develop standards to be used by agencies to protect non-national security oriented computers (the National Security Agency does the same for classified information and national security systems) and requires agencies to develop and implement security programs and plans to protect the information on their computers. The Paperwork Reduction Act of 1995 gives OMB the responsibility to oversee the development and implementation of computer security standards, programs and plans. OMB offers agencies guidance on how to meet their requirements with OMB Circular A-130, Appendix III.

The General Accounting Office (GAO) has found that federal agencies are not consistently good at protecting certain computer systems (typically those used in financial management).[6] GAO has concluded that part of the

---

[5] There is also some debate within the international community about what to do about computer intrusions by government agents; for example, whether such acts would be considered acts of war. For more information regarding this issue, see CRS Report RL30735, *Cyberwarfare*.

[6] U.S. General Accounting Office, *Computer Security. Weaknesses Continue to Place Critical Federal Operations and Assets at Risk*. Testimony before the Subcommittee

problem is that there is not strong government-wide oversight. As part of the FY2001 Defense Authorization Act (P.L. 106-398), Congress passed the Federal Information Security Reform Act. The Act puts into statute much of OMB Circular A-130 guidance. It also strengthens oversight by requiring agencies to have independent reviews of their security programs and plans annually and to report the results of those reviews to OMB. In turn, OMB is to report to Congress on the results.

The security of private-sector computer systems varies. Some industries have been at the forefront of security (e.g. banking and finance), while others are just now appreciating the threat to and vulnerabilities of their systems. In response to PDD-63, some of the sectors that operate critical infrastructures have formed Information Sharing and Analysis Centers (ISACs) and across sectors they have formed the Partnership for Critical Infrastructure Security. The goal of these associations is to learn from each other's experiences and to quickly respond to new attacks and vulnerabilities. It should be noted, too, that in addition to CERT at Carnegie Mellon, individual security firms and security-related associations offer clearinghouses for security-related news, alerts, warnings, etc. The informal network by which security information spreads is also very extensive.

The market for computer and Internet security (divided into hardware, software, and service providers) is large and growing. The CSI/FBI survey cites a 1999 International Data Corporation (IDC) estimate that the security software industry will grow from $2 billion to $7.4 billion by 2003 and the security hardware market will grow from $500 million to $1.9 billion by 2003. According to Redherring.com (Picking the Locks on the Internet Security Market, [http://www/Redherring.com], July 24, 2000), the security services market is expected to grow from $7 billion to $14 billion by 2003. Operating systems and applications developers say they are paying greater attention to designing better security into their products. But still, it is common to have vulnerabilities found in products after they have been put on the market. And, although patches are offered to fix these vulnerabilities in most cases, many system administrators do not keep their software/configurations current. Many intrusions take advantage of vulnerabilities noted many months earlier, for which fixes have already been offered.

There are as yet no industry standards for determining how secure a firm's computer system should be or for assessing how secure it is in fact.

---

on Oversight and Investigations, Committee on Energy and Commerce, House of Representatives. GAO-01-600T. April 5, 2001.

However, there is a push by the major accounting houses and liability forms to make corporate leaders and boards more accountable for their firms' information assets. Also, some observers speculate that it is only a matter of time before owners of computer systems are held responsible for damages done to third-party computers as a result of inadequately protecting their own systems.[7] Nor are there any standards on how secure a vendor's software should be. The federal government, in cooperation with a number of other countries, has developed a set of International Common Criteria for Information Technology Security Evaluation, to allow certified laboratories to test security products and rate their level of security for government use. These criteria may evolve into industry standards for certifying security products.

A number of issues are confronting the 107th Congress during its first session. Congress continues to oversee agencies' performance in meeting their obligations under the Computer Security Act, OMB Circular A-130 and now the Federal Information Security Reform Act. Also, Congress may inquire about the Bush Administration's restructuring of information security coordination. Finally, Congress may face questions about how to strike a balance between its efforts to promote Internet privacy and Internet security. While one cannot protect privacy without security, there are some who fear that without proper checks, efforts to promote security could come at the expense of privacy. On the other hand, as the health care industry and the financial industry prepare to meet new privacy regulations and guidelines, the costs associated with ensuring privacy (via greater access controls, etc.) may become an issue.

A number of bills have been introduced that touch upon one aspect of Internet security or another. H.R. 1259 (Morella) would expand somewhat the responsibilities of the National Institute of Standards and Technology (NIST) in developing computer security standards, to promote the use of commercial security products and to track the use of commercial products by federal agencies. The bill would also require NIST to maintain a list of security products that are certified to conform to standards developed by NIST. It also authorized NIST to perform evaluations of agency information security programs and to report the findings of those evaluations to Congress. H.R. 1292 (Skelton), the Homeland Security Strategy Act of 2001, calls for the President to develop a Homeland Security Strategy that protects the territory, critical infrastructure, and citizens of the United States from the

---

[7] See Computerworld. *IT Security Destined for the Courtroom.* May 21, 2001 Vol 35., No. 21. P. 1,73.

threat or use of chemical, biological, radiological, nuclear, cyber or conventional weapons. H.R. 1158 (Thornberry) would establish a National Homeland Security Agency. The Agency would have transferred to it the authorities, functions, personnel and assets of the Federal Emergency Management Agency, the United States Customs Service, the Border Patrol, the U.S. Coast Guard, the Critical Infrastructure Assurance Office and the National Infrastructure Protection Center. Within the Agency would be a Directorate of Critical Infrastructure that would have responsibility for protecting against cyber attacks. A comparable bill was introduced in the Senate (S. 1534, Lieberman). H.R. 2435 (Davis) provides Freedom of Information Act (FOIA) and anti-trust protections for information relating to computer and network security that is shared with and between the private sector and the federal government. S. 1456 (Bennett) would provide similar protections.

BROADBAND INTERNET ACCESS[8]

Broadband Internet Access gives users the ability to send and receive data at speeds far greater than conventional "dial up" Internet access over existing telephone lines. New broadband technologies – cable modem, digital subscriber line (DSL), satellite, and fixed wireless Internet – are currently being deployed nationwide by the private sector. Concerns in Congress have arisen that while the number of new broadband subscribers continues to grow, the rate of broadband deployment in urban and high-income areas appears to be outpacing deployment in rural and low-income areas, thereby creating a potential "digital divide" in broadband access. The Telecommunications Act of 1996 authorizes the Federal Communications Commission (FCC) to intervene in the telecommunications market if it determines that broadband is not being deployed to all Americans in a "reasonable and timely fashion."

At issue is what, if anything, should be done at the federal level to ensure that broadband deployment is timely, that industry competes on a level playing field, and that service is provided to all sectors of American society. Currently, the debate in Congress centers on three approaches. Those are: 1) easing certain legal restrictions and requirements (imposed by

---

[8] See also CRS Issue Brief IB10045, *Broadband Internet Access: Background and Issues*, by Lennard G. Kruger and Angele A. Gilroy, which is updated more frequently than this report.

the Telecommunications Act of 1996) on incumbent telephone companies that provide high-speed data (broadband) access; 2) compelling cable companies to provide "open access" to competing Internet Service Providers (ISPs); and 3) providing federal financial assistance for broadband deployment in rural and economically disadvantaged areas. Hearings on broadband access in the 107th Congress have been held by a number of congressional committees, including House Commerce, House Judiciary, and House Small Business.

Easing Restrictions and Requirements on Incumbent Telephone Companies

The debate over access to broadband services has prompted policymakers to examine a range of issues to ensure that broadband will be available on a timely and equal basis to all U.S. citizens. One issue under examination is whether present laws and subsequent regulatory policies as they are applied to the ILECs (incumbent local exchange [telephone] companies such as SBC or Verizon (formerly known as Bell Atlantic)) are thwarting the deployment of such services. Two such regulations are the restrictions placed on Bell operating company (BOC) provision of long distance services within their services territories, and network unbundling and resale requirements imposed on all incumbent telephone companies. In the 107th Congress, H.R. 1542 (Tauzin-Dingell) would lift these restrictions and requirements, with some exceptions, for high speed data (broadband) transmission. Whether such requirements are necessary to ensure the development of competition and its subsequent consumer benefits, or are overly burdensome and only discourage needed investment in and deployment of broadband services, continues to be debated. Two other measures (H.R. 1697 and H.R. 1698) introduced in the 107th Congress take a different approach than H.R. 1542. Both measures amend the Clayton Act in an attempt to ensure that markets are open to competition. Meanwhile, in the Senate, two measures (S. 1126 and S. 1127) dealing with broadband deregulation were introduced on June 28, 2001.

Those supporting the lifting or modification of restrictions claim that actions is needed to promote the deployment of broadband services, particularly in rural and under-served areas. Present regulations contained in Sections 271 and 251 of the 1996 Telecommunications Act, they claim, are overburdensome and discourage needed investment in broadband services. According to proponents, unbundling and resale requirements, when applied to advanced services, provide a disincentive for ILECs to upgrade their networks, while BOC and interLATA data restrictions unnecessarily restrict the development of the broadband network. ILECs, they state, are the only entities likely to provide these services in low volume rural and other underserved areas. Therefore, proponents claim, until these regulations are removed, the development and the pace of deployment of broadband technology and services, particularly in unserved areas, will be lacking. Furthermore, supporters state, domination of the Internet backbone market is emerging as a concern and entrance by ILECs (particularly the BOCs) into the market will ensure that competition will thrive with no single or small group of providers dominating. Proponents also cite the need for regulatory parity; cable companies who serve approximately 70 percent of the broadband market are not subject to these requirements. Additional concerns that the lifting of restrictions on data would remove BOC incentives to open up the local loop to gain interLATA relief for voice services are also unfounded, they state. The demand by consumers for bundled services and the large and lucrative nature of the long distance voice market will, according to proponents, provide the necessary incentives for BOCs to seek relief for interLATA voice services.

On the other hand, opponents claim that the lifting of restrictions and requirements will undermine the incentives needed to ensure that the BOCs and the other ILECs will open up their networks to competition. Present restrictions, opponents claim, were built into the 1996 Telecommunications Act to help ensure that competition will develop in the provision of telecommunications services. Modification of these regulations, critics claim, will remove the incentives needed to open up the "monopoly" in the provision of local services. Competitive safeguards such as unbundling and resale are necessary, opponents claim, to ensure that competitors will have access to the "monopoly bottleneck" last mile to the customer. Therefore, they state the enactment of legislation to modify these provisions of the 1996 Telecommunications Act will all but stop the growth of competition in the provision of local telephone service. A major change in existing regulations, opponents claim, would not only remove the incentives needed to open up the local loop but would likely result in the financial ruin of providers attempting to offer competition to incumbent local exchange carriers. As a result, consumers will be hurt, critics claim, since the hope-for benefits of competition such as increased consumer choice and lower rates will never emerge. Concern over the inability of regulators to distinguish between provision of voice-only and data services if BOC interLATA restrictions for data services and ILEC unbundling and resale requirements for advanced services are lifted was also expressed. Opponents also dismiss arguments that BOC entrance into the marketplace is needed to ensure competition. The marketplace, opponents claim, is a dynamic one but proposed deregulation would unsettle nascent competition in the market.

Open Access

Legislation introduced in the 106th Congress sought to compel cable companies that provide broadband access give "open access" to all ISPs. In effect, the legislation would have enabled cable broadband customers to subscribe to their ISP of choice without first going through their cable provider's ISP. At issue is whether cable networks should be required to share their lines with, and give equal treatment to, rival ISPs who wish to sell their services to consumers. Supporters argue that open access is necessary to prevent cable companies from creating "closed networks," limiting access to content, and stifling competition. Opponents of open access counter that an open access mandate would inhibit the cable industry's ongoing nationwide investment in broadband technology, and assert that healthy competition does and will exist in the form of alternate broadband technologies such as DSL and satellites.

The arguments for and against open access have been heard on the local level, as cities, counties, and states have taken up the issue of whether to mandate open access requirements on local cable franchises. In June 1999, a federal judge ruled that the city of Portland, OR, had the right to require open access to the Tele-Communications Incorporated (TCI) broadband network as a condition for transferring its local cable television franchise to AT&T. AT&T appealed the ruling to the U.S. Court of Appeals for the Ninth Circuit. On June 22, 2000, the Court ruled in favor of AT&T, thereby reversing the earlier ruling. The court ruled that high-speed Internet access via a cable modem is defined as a "telecommunications service," and not subject to direct regulation by local franchising authorities.

The debate thus moves to the federal level, where many interpret the Court's decision as giving the FCC authority to regulate broadband cable services as a "telecommunications service." However, the FCC also has the authority *not* to regulate if it determines that such action is unnecessary to prevent discrimination and protect consumers. To date, the FCC has chosen *not* to mandate open access, citing the infancy of cable broadband service and the current and future availability of competitive technologies such as DSL and satellite broadband services. However, in light of the June 22 court decision, the FCC announced on June 30, 2000, that it will conduct a formal proceeding to determine whether or not cable-Internet service should be regulated as a telecommunications service, and whether the FCC should mandate open access nationwide. On September 28, 2000, the FCC formally issued a Notice of Inquiry (NOI) which will explore whether or not the Commission should require access to cable and other high-speed systems by ISPs. Meanwhile, recent developments within the cable industry could have an impact on the open access debate. On January 10,2000, AOL announced plans to merge with time Warner, Inc. Now approved by the federal government, the merger gives AOL access to the second-largest cable television system in the United States, and a share in Roadrunner, one of the two major cable modem ISPs. On December 14, 2000, the Federal Trade Commission announced its approval of the AOL Time Warner merger with conditions. Under the terms of the proposed consent order, AOL Time Warner is required to open its cable systems to competing ISPs, and prohibited from interfering with the content passed along the bandwidth contracted for by non-affiliated ISPs. On January 11, 2001, the FCC announced its approval of the merger with additional conditions intended to promote open access.

Federal Assistance for Broadband Deployment

Other legislation introduced in the 107th Congress would provide tax credits and grant/loan guarantees for broadband deployment primarily in rural and/or low income areas. The Senate version of the farm bill – S. 1628 (Harkin) – contains language authorizing the Secretary of Agriculture to provide grants and loans to eligible entities providing broadband service in rural areas. S. 1628 would authorize a funding level of $100 million per year for five years. Meanwhile, a broadband tax credit provision has been added to the Senate Finance Committee version of the economic stimulus bill, H.R. 3090 (Economic Security and Recovery Act of 2001). Modeled on S. 88 (the Broadband Internet Access Act introduced by Senator Rockefeller), section 902 of H.R. 3090 would provide a 10% credit for deploying "current generation" broadband equipment in rural and underserved areas and for all residential broadband subscribers.

ELECTRONIC COMMERCE[9]

Background

The convergence of computer and telecommunications technologies has revolutionized how we get, store, retrieve, and share information. Many experts contend that this convergence has created the Information Economy, driven by the Internet, and fueled a surge in U.S. productivity and economic growth. Commercial transactions on the Internet, whether retail business-to-consumer or business-to-business, are commonly called electronic commerce, or "e-commerce."

Since the mid-1990s, commercial transactions on the Internet have grown substantially.[10] By 1996, Internet traffic, including e-commerce, was doubling every 100 days. By mid-1997, the U.S. Department of Commerce reported that just over 4 million people were using e-commerce; by the end of 1997, that figure had grown to over 10 million users. In May 2001 the Bureau of the Census, in the Department of Commerce, reported that for the first quarter of 2001, U.S. e-commerce sales hit $6.99 billion – up 33.5% from the first quarter of 2000, but down 19% from the fourth quarter of 2000. (This would be the first decline in six quarters, or since the fourth quarter of 1999, when the Bureau of the Census started recording such data). Business conducted over the Internet continues to grow, even with an economic slowdown and with many new "dot-com" businesses no longer in existence. The Forrester Research Group released a report in March 2001 that estimated 2000 world e-commerce at $657 billion, with a projected growth to $6.8 trillion. The consulting firm IDC reported an estimated $354 billion in e-commerce sales in 2000, with a projected growth to $5 trillion in 2005. What these reports, and others like them, indicate is how difficult it is to precisely measure e-commerce on a macroeconomic scale, other than to say that it is likely that strong growth, particularly of e-commerce sales in the global economy, will continue over the long term.

---

[9] See also CRS Report RS20426, *Electronic Commerce: An Introduction*, by Glenn J. McLoughlin, which is updated more frequently than this report.

[10] For statistics and other data on e-commerce, see: CRS Report RL30435, *Internet and E-Commerce Statistics: What They Mean and Where to Find Them On the Web*. Other sources include: [http://www.idc.com], [http://www.abcnews.go.com], [http://www.forrester.com], [http://www.emarketer.com], and [http://www.cs.cmu.edu]. It is important to note that some measurements of e-commerce, particularly that data reported in the media, have not been verified.

Internationally, there are issues regarding Internet use and e-commerce growth. While the western industrialized nations dominate Internet development and use, by the year 2003 more than half of the material posted on the Internet will be in a language other than English. This has large ramifications for e-commerce and ease of transactions, security and privacy issues. Policymakers, industry leaders, academicians, and others are concerned that this development will not correlate with equal access to the Internet for many in developing nations – therefore creating a global "digital divide." The United States and Canada represent the largest percentage of Internet users, at 56.6%. Europe follows with 23.4%. At the end of 2000, of approximately 200 million Internet users worldwide, only 3.1% are in Latin America, 0.5% are in the Middle East, and 0.6% are in Africa. The Asian Pacific region has 15.8% of all Internet users; but its rate of growth of Internet use is nearly twice as fast as the United States and Canada. In this respect, the U.S.-Canada share of Internet use may decline to 36% by 2005.

The E-Commerce Industry

Even with some concern about accuracy and timeliness of e-commerce statistics, reliable industry source report huge jumps in e-commerce transactions, particularly during fourth quarter holiday shopping. But long-term, industry growth has not been limited to just holiday shopping. According to a study undertaken by the University of Texas, the Internet portion of the U.S. economy grew at a compounded rate of 174% from 1995-1998 (the U.S. gross domestic product grew at 2.8% during the same period), and e-commerce accounted for one-third of that growth. Increasingly, many firms use "vortals" – vertically integrated portals or gateways that advertise or provide information on a specific industry or special interest. As a portion of e-commerce business, vortals provide targeted advertising for e-commerce transactions, and may grow from 35% of all e-commerce advertising to 57% by 2004. However, not all firms providing these services are profitable; in fact, most have yet to turn a profit.

One of the fastest growing sectors of e-commerce is business-to-business transactions – what is often called "B2B." This sector continues to expand, even in the current economic downturn. The Forrester Group, a private sector consulting firm, estimates that by 2003, that sector of the U.S. economy will reach $1.5 trillion, up from nearly $200 billion in 2000. Business-to-business transactions between small and medium sized businesses and their suppliers is rapidly growing, as many of these firms

Clinton Administration Policies: 1998-2001

The Clinton Administration advocated a wide range of policy prescriptions to encourage e-commerce growth. These included calling on the World Trade Organization (WTO) to declare the Internet to be a tax-free environment for delivering both goods and services; recommending that no new tax policies be imposed on Internet commerce; stating that nations develop a "uniform commercial code" for electronic commerce; requesting that intellectual property protection – patents, trademarks, and copyrights – be consistent and enforceable; that nations adhere to international agreements to protect the security and privacy of Internet commercial transactions; that governments and businesses cooperate to more fully develop and expand the Internet infrastructure; and that businesses self-regulate e-commerce content.

The Clinton Administration's "The Emerging Digital Economy" (April 1998), "The Emerging Digital Economy II" (June 1999), "Digital Economy 2000" (June 2000), and "Leadership for the New Millennium, Delivering on Digital Progress and Prosperity" (January 2001) provided overarching views on domestic and global e-commerce. These reports provide data on the explosive growth of e-commerce, its role in global trade and national Gross Domestic Product (GDP), and contributions that computer and telecommunications technology convergence is making to productivity gains in the United States and worldwide. The Administration also argued that the effects that information technologies have had on raising national productivity, lowering inflation, creating high wage jobs, and contributing up to one-third of all domestic growth in the 1990s.

Issues for the Bush Administration and the 107th Congress

Since the mid-1990s, Congress also has taken an active interest in e-commerce issues. Among the many issues, Congress may revisit policies that establish federal encryption procedures and provide electronic security in the wake of September 11, 2001. The 107th Congress has passed a bill that would extend the moratorium on domestic e-commerce taxation to

November 2003. In addition, congressional policymakers are looking at the European Union (EU) and WTO policies and regulations in e-commerce.

Protection and Security Issues

There are a variety of protection and security issues that affect e-commerce growth and development. Encryption is the encoding of electronic messages to transfer important information and data, in which "keys" are needed to unlock or decode the message. Encryption is an important element of e-commerce security, with the issue of who holds the keys at the core of the debate. Until 1998, the Clinton Administration promoted the use of strong (greater than 56 bits) encryption domestically and abroad only if the encryption product had "key recovery" features in which a "key recovery agent" holds a "spare key" to decrypt the information. Under this policy, the Clinton Administration tried to use export control policy to influence companies to develop key recovery encryption products. There was no control over domestic use of encrypted products, but the Clinton Administration hoped that companies would not want to develop two sets of encryption products, one for the United States and another for the rest of the world. However, businesses and consumer groups opposed this approach. For many U.S. businesses, the Clinton Administration export policy had the potential to impede their efforts to become part of the growing e-commerce global phenomena by forcing them to create two versions of the same product. Consumer groups opposed government policies determining who would have access to spare keys.

In September 1999, the United States announced plans to further relax its encryption export policy by allowing export of unlimited key length encryption products, with some exception. It also advocated reduced reporting requirements for those firms that export encrypted products. The rules for implementing this policy were issued in September 2000 by the Bureau of Export Administration in the Department of Commerce. However, the events of September 11, 2001 have caused many in industry and government to review this policy – and the USA PATRIOT Act of 2001 (P.L. 107-56) has given lawmakers greater authority to gain access to electronic financial transactions (for example, to ferret out illegal money laundering). Consumers and civil liberties activists are very concerned about this development and have said they will monitor this law closely.

In a related area, in 2000 Congress considered and passed legislation establishing standards for transmission and verification of electronic transmissions. *Electronic signatures* are a means of verifying the identity of the user of a computer system to control access to, or to authorize, a transaction. The main congressional interests in electronic signatures focus on enabling electronic signatures to carry legal weight in place of written signatures, removing the inconsistencies among state policies that some fear may retard the growth of e-commerce, and establishing federal government requirements for use of electronic signatures when filing information electronically. Neither federal law enforcement nor national security agencies oppose these objectives, and most U.S. businesses would like a national electronic signatures standard to further enhance e-commerce. When President Clinton signed into law the Electronic Signatures in Global and National Commerce Act (P.L. 106-229), the process of developing national electronic signature standards was begun. Among its many provisions, this law also establishes principles for U.S. negotiations to follow for setting global electronic signatures policies.

E-Commerce Taxation

Congress passed the Internet Tax Freedom Act on October 21, 1998, as Titles XI and XII of the Omnibus Consolidated and Emergency Supplemental Appropriations Act of 1999 (P.L. 105-277, 112 Stat 2681). Among its provisions, the Act imposes a 3-year moratorium on the ability of state and local governments to levy certain taxes on the Internet; it prohibits taxes on Internet access, unless such a tax was generally imposed and actually enforced prior to October 1, 1998; it creates an Advisory Commission on Electronic Commerce (ACEC), which may make recommendations to Congress on e-commerce taxation in the United States and abroad; and it opposes regulatory, tariff, and tax barriers to international e-commerce and asks the President to pursue international agreements to ban them. The ACEC made its policy recommendations, after much debate and some divisiveness, to Congress on April 3, 2000. The ACEC called for, among its recommendations, extending the domestic Internet tax moratorium for five more years, through 2006; prohibiting the taxation of digitized goods over the Internet, regardless of national source; and a continued moratorium on any international tariffs on electronic transmissions over the Internet.

Congressional interest in Internet taxation has weighed concerns about impeding the growth of e-commerce by taxing revenues; enforcement and compliance of an Internet tax; and policies outside of the United States which do not impose an Internet tax. H.R. 1552, The Internet Tax Nondiscrimination Act (Rep. Cox) would extend the Internet tax moratorium through November 1, 2003. It was passed by the House of Representatives on October 16, 2001 and passed by the Senate on November 15, 2001. It awaits President Bush's signature.

The EU and WTO

While much of the debate on the government's role in e-commerce has focused on domestic issues in the United States, two important players – the EU and the WTO – will likely have an important impact on global e-commerce policy development. The EU is very active in e-commerce issues. In some areas there is agreement with U.S. policies, and in some areas there are still tensions. While the EU as an entity represents a sizable portion of global Internet commerce, across national boundaries, Internet use and e-commerce potential varies widely. Supporters state that e-commerce policy should not be set by EU bureaucrats in Brussels. Therefore, the EU has approached e-commerce with what one observer has called a "light regulatory touch." Among contentious issues, the EU has supported the temporary moratorium on global e-commerce taxes, and supports making the moratorium permanent. But the EU has taken a different approach than U.S. policy by treating electronic transmissions (including those that deliver electronic transmissions – including e-commerce – as services, making them subject to EU value-added duties. The EU also has taken a different approach to data protection and privacy, key components for strengthening e-commerce security and maintaining consumer confidence. The EU actions prohibit the transfer of data in and out of the EU, unless the outside country provides sufficient privacy safeguards. The U.S. position is to permit industry self-regulation of data protection and privacy safeguards. The WTO has presented another set of challenges to U.S. policymakers. The first two WTO ministerial meetings addressed issues that have an impact on e-commerce. The first WTO Ministerial conference was held in Singapore on December 9-13, 1996. Among the issues considered by the WTO participants was an agreement to reduce trade barriers for information technology goods and services. This issue was considered vital to the development of telecommunications infrastructure – including the Internet – among developing nations. A majority of participants signed an agreement to reduce these barriers. At the second WTO Ministerial conference, held in Geneva on May 18 and 20, 1998, an agreement was reached by the participating trade ministers to direct the WTO General Council to develop a work program on electronic commerce and to report on the progress of the work program, with recommendations, at the next conference. The ministers also agreed that countries continue the practice of not imposing tariffs on electronic transmissions. Since then, e-commerce taxation and Internet access issues continue to be discussed at WTO staff and ministerial meetings.

UNSOLICITED COMMERCIAL ELECTRONIC MAIL ("JUNK E-MAIL" OR "SPAM")[11]

One aspect of increased use of the Internet for electronic mail (e-mail) has been the advent of unsolicited commercial e-mail (UCE), also called junk e-mail, spam, or unsolicited bulk e-mail. *The Report to the Federal Trade Commission of the Ad-Hoc Working Group on Unsolicited Commercial Email* [http://www.cdt.org/spam] reviews the issues in this debate.

In 1991, Congress passed the Telephone Consumer Protection Act (P.L. 102-243) that prohibits, *inter alia*, unsolicited advertising via facsimile machines, or "junk fax". Many question whether there should be an analogous law for computers, or at least some method for letting a consumer know before opening an e-mail message whether or not it is unsolicited advertising and to direct the sender to cease transmission of such messages. At a November 3, 1999 hearing of the House Commerce telecommunications subcommittee, a representative of the SBC Internet Services, a subsidiary of SBC Communications, Inc., stated that 35% of all the e-mail transmitted over SBC's Internet systems in its Pacific Bell and Southwestern Bell regions is UCE.

Opponents of junk e-mail such as the Coalition Against Commercial Email (CAUCE) argue that not only is junk e-mail annoying, but its cost is borne by consumers, not marketers. Consumers are charged higher fees by ISPs that must invest resources to upgrade equipment to manage the high volume of e-mail, deal with customer complaints, and mount legal challenges to junk e-mailers. CAUCE's founder, Ray Everett-Church, is cited in the January 31, 2001 edition of *Newsday* as saying that some ISPs estimate that spam costs consumers about $2-3 per month. Some want to prevent bulk e-mailers from sending messages to anyone with whom they do not have an established business relationship, treating junk e-mail the same way as junk fax. Proponents of unsolicited commercial e-mail argue that it is

---

[11] See also CRS Report RS20037, *"Junk E-Mail": An Overview of Issues and Legislation Concerning Unsolicited Commercial Electronic Mail ("Spam")*, by Marcia S. Smith, which is updated more frequently than this report.

a valid method of advertising. The Direct Marketing Association (DMA), for example, argues that instead of banning unsolicited commercial e-mail, individuals should be given the opportunity to notify the sender of the message that they want to be removed from its mailing list – or "opt-out." In January 2000, the DMA launched a new service, the E-mail Preference Service, where any of its members that send UCE must do so through a special Web site where consumers who wish to "opt out" of receiving such mail can register themselves [http://www.e-mps.org]. Each DMA member is required to check its list of intended recipients and to delete those consumers who have opted out. While acknowledging that the service will not stop all spam, the DMA considers it "part of the overall solution" (see [http://www.the-dma.org/aboutdma/release4.shtml]). Critics argue that most spam does not come from DMA members, so the DMA plan is insufficient.

To date, the issue of restraining junk e-mail has been fought primarily over the Internet or in the courts. Some ISPs will return junk e-mail to its origin, and groups opposed to junk e-mail will send blasts of e-mail to a mass e-mail company, disrupting the company's computer systems. Filtering software also is available to screen out e-mail based on keywords or return addresses. Knowing this, mass e-mailers may avoid certain keywords or continually change addresses to foil the software, however. In the courts, ISPs with unhappy customers and businesses that believe their reputations have been tarnished by misrepresentations in junk e-mail have brought suit against mass e-mailers.

Although several bills were debated in both the 105th and 106th Congresses, no legislation cleared Congress. Some states are passing their own legislation. According to the National Conference of State Legislatures, as of March 2000, 15 states had enacted such laws and 16 introduced spam bills during their 2000 legislative sessions. The 107th congress remains interested in the issue at the federal level. Five bills have been introduced to date: H.R. 95 (Green), H.R. 718 (Wilson), H.R. 1017 (Goodlatte), H.R. 3146 (C. Smith), and S. 630 (Burns). H.R. 2472 (Lofgren) is not a spam bill per se, but would require marks or notices on e-mail forwarded to minors that contains sexually oriented advertising. H.R. 718 has been reported from the House Energy and Commerce Committee (H.Rept. 107-41, Part 1) and the House Judiciary Committee (H.Rept. 107-41, Part 2). The two versions are quite different.

INTERNET DOMAIN NAMES[12]

The 107th Congress continues to monitor issues related to the Internet domain name system (DNS). Internet domain names were created to provide users with a simple location name for computers on the Internet, rather than using the more complex, unique Internet Protocol (IP) number that designates their specific location. As the Internet has grown, the method for allocating and designating domain names has become increasingly controversial.

The Internet originated with research funding provided by the Department of Defense Advanced Research Projects Agency (DARPA) to establish a military network. As its use expanded, a civilian segment evolved with support from the National Science Foundation (NSF) and other science agencies. No formal statutory authorities or international agreements govern the management and operation of the Internet and the DNS. Prior to 1993, NSF was responsible for registration of nonmilitary generic Top Level Domains (gTLDs) such as .com, .org, and .net. In 1993, the NSF entered into a 5-year cooperative agreement with Network Solutions, Inc. (NSI) to operate Internet domain name registration services. With the cooperative agreement between NSI and NSF due to expire in 1998, the Clinton Administration, through the Department of Commerce (DOC), began exploring ways to transfer administration of the DNS to the private sector.

In the wake of much discussion among Internet stakeholders, and after extensive public comment on a previous proposal, the DOC, on June 5, 1998, issued a final statement of policy, *Management of Internet Names and Addresses* (also known as the "White Paper"). The White Paper stated that the U.S. government was prepared to recognize and enter into agreement with "a new not-for-profit corporation formed by private sector Internet stakeholders to administer policy for the Internet name and address system." On October 2, 1998, the DOC accepted a proposal for an Internet Corporation for Assigned Names and Numbers (ICANN). On November 25, 1998, DOC and ICANN signed an official Memorandum of Understanding (MOU), whereby DOC and ICANN agreed to jointly design, develop, and test the mechanisms, methods, and procedures necessary to transition management responsibility for DNS functions to a private-sector not-for-profit entity.

---

[12] See also CRS Report 97-868, *Internet Domain Names: Background and Policy Issues*, by Lennard G. Kruger, which is updated more frequently than this report.

The White Paper also signaled DOC's intention to ramp down the government's Cooperative Agreement with NSI, with the objective of introducing competition into the domain name space while maintaining stability and ensuring an orderly transition. During this transition period, government obligations will be terminated as DNS responsibilities are transferred to ICANN. Specifically, NSI committed to a timetable for development of a Shared Registration System that permits multiple registrars to provide registration services within the .com, .net, and .org gTLDs. NSI (now VeriSign) will continue to administer the root server system until receiving further instruction from the government.

Significant disagreements between NSI on the one hand, and ICANN and DOC on the other, arose over how a successful and equitable transition would be made from NSI's previous status as exclusive registrar of .com, .org, and .net domain names, to a system that allows multiple and competing registrars. On November 10, 1999, ICANN, NSI, and DOC formally signed an agreement which provided that NSI (now VeriSign) was required to sell its registrar operation by May 10, 2001 in order to retain control of the dot-com registry until 2007. In April 2001, arguing that the registrar business in now highly competitive, VeriSign reached a new agreement with ICANN whereby its registry and registrar businesses would not have to be separated. With DOC approval, ICANN and VeriSign will continue to operate the .org registry until 2002; the .net registry until June 30, 2005 (which prior to that time will be opened for recompetition unless market measurements indicate that an earlier expiration date is necessary for competitive reasons); and the .com registry until at least the expiration date of the current agreement in 2007, and possibly beyond. VeriSign agreed to enhanced measures (including annual audits arranged by ICANN and made available to the U.S. government) to ensure that its registry-operation unit gives equal treatment to all domain name registrars, including VeriSign's registrar business.

Meanwhile, on September 4, 2000, ICANN and the DOC agreed to extend their MOU until September 30, 2001 or sooner, if both parties agree that the work set under the MOU has been completed. The MOU has subsequently been extended to September 30, 2002. Remaining tasks, many of which are underway, include: creating new Internet top-level domains, completing selection of the ICANN Board of Directors, enhancing the architecture of the root-name server system, formalizing contractual relationships between ICANN and the regional Internet Protocol address registries, and establishing stable arrangements between ICANN and the organizations responsible for the operation of country-code Top-Level Domains (TLDs).

Until the full transition to a private sector-controlled DNS system is completed, the DOC remains responsible for monitoring the extent to which ICANN satisfies the principles of the White Paper as it makes critical DNS decisions. Congress remains keenly interested in how the Administration manages and oversees the transition to private sector ownership of the DNS. Meanwhile, criticism of ICANN has grown, with some pointing to the recent ICANN-VeriSign agreement as an example of how ICANN remains more responsive to corporate interests than to Internet users.

Two key issues addressed by ICANN are the addition of new top level domains and the election of At-Large Board members. Additional TLDs could significantly expand the number of domain names available for registration by the public. At its November 16, 2000 annual meeting, ICANN selected seven companies or organizations to operate a registry for one of seven new TLDs, as follows: .biz, .aero, .name, .pro, .museum, .info, and .coop. Both .info and .biz became operational on October 1 and November 6, 2001 respectively, while the five other chosen TLDs are in various stages of the process toward becoming operational.

ICANN's selection of new TLDs has proven controversial. Critics assert that the TLD selection process was inappropriately subjective, insufficiently transparent and lacking in adequate due process procedures. In its defense, ICANN argues that the selection process was sufficient to meet its goal of expeditiously selecting a limited number of diverse TLDs, and that these will serve as an initial and experimental "proof of concept" phase in order to ensure that new TLDs can be introduced in the future without undermining the stability of the Internet. Both the House Energy and Commerce and the Senate Commerce, Science, and Transportation Committees held hearings in February 2001 to scrutinize ICANN and its TLD selection process. In August 2001, the Chairmen and Ranking Members of the Energy and Commerce Committee and the Telecommunications Subcommittee sent a letter to the Secretary of Commerce urging DOC to encourage ICANN to speed its process for selecting additional TLDs. Meanwhile, legislation introduced by Representative Shimkus on June 28, 2001 (H.R. 2417) would direct DOC to compel ICANN to create a "kids-friendly top level domain name." On November 1, 2001, the House Energy and Commerce Committee held a hearing on H.R. 2417 and considered proposed substitute language that would direct DOC to create a second-level .kids domain within the .us country code TLD. The .us domain is controlled by the DOC, which recently contracted its operation to a private company, NeuStar, which has also proposed the creation of a .kids domain as part of its contract with DOC. At the hearing, the DOC expressed some reservations about the revised H.R.

2417, namely that DOC would be required to develop and enforce content standards, and that the legislation alters the existing contractual obligations between DOC and NeuStar.

Regarding the composition of ICANN's board of directors, ICANN bylaws call for an international and geographically diverse 19-member board of directors, composed of a president, nine at-large members, and nine members nominated by three Supporting Organizations representing Domain Name, Address, Internet Protocol constituencies. During October 1999, the three Supporting Organizations each selected three directors for the permanent board. The nine new directors joined the ten sitting interim directors, who were to serve until an additional nine directors were elected to the permanent board by ICANN's At-Large membership. At ICANN's March 2000 meeting in Cairo, the sitting board agreed to a plan whereby five At-Large board members, one from each of five geographic regions of the world, would be directly elected by Internet users. On October 10, 2000 ICANN announced the five new At-Large board members elected by over 34,000 Internet users. At the November 2000 annual meeting, ICANN initiated a study to determine how to select the remaining At-Large board members. Meanwhile, the sitting board has extended the terms of four of its interim members until 2002 to serve with the five newly elected At-Large board members. The At-Large Membership Study Committee (ALSC) released its report and recommendations on November 5, 2001. The ALSC is recommending that only domain name holders be eligible to vote for at-large board members, and that the number of at-large members on the board be reduced from nine to six. The ALSC recommendations will likely be considered by the board at ICANN's March 2002 meeting in Ghana. In the wake of the September 11 terrorist attack, ICANN's November 2001 meeting (in Marina del Rey, California) was redirected to focus almost entirely on the security of the DNS.

Another issue surrounding the DNS is the resolution of trademark disputes that arise in designating domain names. In the early years of the Internet, when the primary users were academic institutions and government agencies, little concern existed over trademarks and domain names. As the Internet grew, however, the fastest growing number of requests for domain names were in the .com domain because of the explosion of businesses offering products and services on the Internet. Since domain names have been available from NSI on a first-come, first-serve basis, some companies discovered that their name had already been registered. The situation was aggravated by some people (dubbed "cybersquatters") registering domain names in the hope that they might be able to sell them to companies that place a high value on them.

The increase in conflicts over property rights to certain trademarked names has resulted in a number of lawsuits. The White Paper called upon the World Intellectual Property Organization (WIPO) to develop a set of recommendations for trademark/domain name dispute resolutions, and to submit those recommendations to ICANN. At ICANN's August 1999 meeting in Santiago, the board of directors adopted a uniform dispute resolution policy (UDRP) to be applied by all ICANN-accredited registrars. Under this policy, registrars receiving complaints will take no action until receiving instructions from the domain-name holder or an order of a court or arbitrator. An exception is made for "abusive registrations" (i.e. cybersquatting or cyberpiracy), whereby a special administrative procedure (conducted largely online by a neutral panel, lasting 45 days or less, and costing about $1000) will resolve the dispute. Implementation of ICANN's Domain Name Dispute Resolution Policy commenced on December 9, 1999. Meanwhile, the 106th Congress took action, passing the Anticybersquatting Consumer Protection Act (incorporated into P.L. 106-113, the FY2000 Consolidated Appropriations Act). The Act gives courts the authority to order the forfeiture, cancellation, and/or transfer of domain names registered in "bad faith" that are identical or similar to trademarks. The bill also provides for statutory civil damages of at least $1,000, but not more than $100,000, per domain name identifier.

WIPO has initiated a second study which will produce recommendations on how to resolve disputes over bad faith, abusive, misleading or unfair use of other types of domain names such as personal names, geographical terms, names of international organizations, and others. WIPO released its second report on September 3, 2001, recommending that generic drug names be canceled upon complaint that international intergovernmental organization names be subject to a dispute resolution process. However, WIPO did not recommend new rules regarding personal, geographical, or trade names. WIPO has decided to subject its second report to a comprehensive analysis by its Standing Committee on the Law of Trademarks, Industrial Designs and Geographical Indications. The analysis is expected to be completed by mid-2002.

GOVERNMENT INFORMATION TECHNOLOGY MANAGEMENT[13]

The growing role of the Internet in the political economy of the United States has attracted increased congressional attention to government information technology management issues. Interest has been further heightened by national information infrastructure development efforts and e-government initiatives. Although wide-ranging, government information technology management issues can be characterized by three major themes: infrastructure development, resource management, and the provision of online services (e-government). Each of these is likely to be addressed by the 107th Congress.

Internet Infrastructure and National Policy

Since 1995, when the Internet first came into prominence, the question of who should maintain and expand the U.S. information infrastructure has been raised by many policymakers. The Clinton Administration articulated its support of federal technology policy in the 1992 campaign, including the rapid expansion of telecommunications-based "information superhighways." Again, during the 1996 presidential campaign, President Clinton and Vice President Gore contended that investment in advanced technology would strengthen the U.S. economy by creating jobs and address pressing social problems. Early in the Clinton Administration, several policy proposals were presented to Congress that articulated a vision of how telecommunication technologies, services, and applications could be combined in a national information network. This concept was to interconnect businesses, governments, researchers, educators, and the general public with advanced telecommunications networks and a diverse multitude of information resources.

Until the 106th Congress, most policymakers tended to respond to the Clinton Administration's policies, rather than provide a specific policy or program alternative. However, in the 106th Congress, several Members of Congress presented their approaches to support a national information infrastructure that would enable all Americans to access information and

---

[13] See also CRS Report RL30661, *Government Information Technology Management: Past and Future Issues (the Clinger-Cohen Act)*, by Jeffrey W. Seifert.

communicate with each other using voice, data, image or video at anytime, anywhere. Among these legislative initiatives was the Networking and Information Technology Research Development Act (H.R. 2086, Sensenbrenner), which would have doubled existing federal computing research programs, including developing new Internet-related technologies, over a five-year period. While this bill was not passed by Congress, this and other legislative initiatives reflected greater congressional interest in addressing those areas of Internet research and development not currently undertaken by U.S. industry, but might be vital to the Internet's future growth.

Information Technology R&D

For FY2001, most federal Internet research and development is part of a large government effort to support a wide range of related scientific research and technology development. This is called the Information Technology (IT) Research and Development initiative, and includes a wide range of programs, from software upgrades at federal agencies to high performance computing developments. The total funding for federal IT Research & Development in FY2001 is $2.1 billion. The National Science Foundation received a significant increase in its IT research and development budget, going from $90 million in FY2000 to $215 million in FY2001. The Department of Energy has the largest federal IT research and development budget, at $657 million, which includes both civilian and defense IT efforts. Finally, an important component of the federal IT Research and Development initiative is the Next Generation Internet (NGI) program. The NGI is a multi-agency effort to develop new Internet research and applications that will assist federal agencies which have research and development as one of their missions. For FY2001, the six federal agencies in the NGI program will receive a total of $89 million.

Information Resource Management: The Role of a Federal CIO[14]

Debate over the creation of a federal Chief Information Officer (CIO) position has ebbed and flowed in Congress over the past five years. In private sector organizations with a CIO, this person serves as the senior decisionmaker providing leadership and direction for information resource development, procurement, and management with a focus on improving efficiency and the quality of services delivered. Creating a federal CIO position was originally considered in an early draft of what became the Clinger-Cohen Act in 1995 (P.L. 104-106), but the idea was dropped in favor of creating CIO positions within individual executive branch agencies. The CIO Council was later established in 1996 by Executive Order 13011 as a forum for agency CIOs and Deputy CIOs to share information and improve government information resource management practices. The mixed results of agency-level CIOs, combined with a growing interest in better managing government technology resources, brought renewed attention to creating a single federal CIO position, or a "national CIO," during the 106th Congress. In addition, the recent piecemeal efforts to move government functions and services online has led some observers to call for an "e-government czar" or a national CIO to coordinate these efforts.

Although there appears to be a growing bipartisan consensus regarding the need for a federal CIO, issues such as the organizational location and the scope of responsibility are still the subject of debate. The placement of the federal CIO is perhaps the most hotly contested issue. Specifically, there is disagreement over whether the federal CIO should be placed in the Office of Management and Budget (OMB) or if a new office should be established within the White House to focus solely on information technology issues. In September 2000, the House Government Reform Committee's Subcommittee on Government Management, Information, and Technology held a hearing regarding two bills proposed by Representatives Turner and Davis earlier that summer (discussed below). Much of the testimony focused on the relationship between the proposed federal CIO and the OMB. Then-Deputy Director of Management at OMB, Sally Katzen, argued that situating oversight of information technology management within OMB's management and budgeting authority was essential for the successful

---

[14] See also CRS Report 30914, *Federal Chief Information Officer (CIO): Opportunities and Challenges,* by Jeffery W. Seifert, which is updated more frequently than this report.

budgeting and execution of information technology programs. In response, critics of this approach argued that IT programs are crucial enough to warrant autonomous management and budget authority by specialists who can devote their full energy to the success of government IT projects. Some observers suggest there are lessons to be learned from the lackluster results of the agency-level CIO provisions in the Clinger-Cohen Act. In reviews of this provision, the GAO has cited the divided attention of agency-level CIOs with multiple spheres of responsibility as an obstacle for implementing information technology management reforms. The GAO has further stated that the role of the CIO is a full-time leadership position requiring complete attention to information resource management issues.[15]

Another issue that has received less attention is the scope of responsibility of the proposed federal CIO. Specifically, questions have been raised about oversight of government information security. Some proponents suggest that the federal CIO should be empowered to develop and implement a comprehensive response to information security threats. Critics of this approach argue that individual agencies may believe they have a reduced obligation or will devote fewer resources to information security at a time when threats to information resources are climbing.

During the 106th Congress, legislation was introduced in the House calling for the establishment of a federal CIO position. One bill (H.R. 4670, Turner) would have created a federal CIO in an office outside of OMB, established a CIO Council by law rather than by executive order, and made the CIO head of the Council. A second bill (H.R. 5024, Davis) would have created a White House Office of Information Policy to be headed by a federal CIO, with a broad mandate to create federal IT policy, a staff, an authorized budget to carry out the duties of a federal CIO, and the power to coordinate and execute government-wide information security efforts. Neither bill was passed in the last Congress; however, these issues are being revisited in the 107th Congress.

On May 1, 2001, Senator Lieberman introduced S. 803, the E-Government Act of 2001. Among its many provisions, S. 803 calls for the establishment of a federal CIO, to be appointed by the President and confirmed by the Senate. The federal CIO would be in charge of a proposed Office of Information Policy and would report to the Director of OMB. S. 803 would also establish the CIO Council by law with the federal CIO as

---

[15] General Accounting Office, *Chief Information Officers: Ensuring Strong Leadership and an Effective Council*, GAO-T-AIMD-98-22, 27 October 1997. General Accounting Office, *VA Information Technology: Improvements Needed to Implement Legislative Reforms*, GAO/AIMD-98-154, 7 July 1998.

Chair. This bill has been referred to the Governmental Affairs Committee, which held a hearing on the bill on July 11, 2001. Also on July 11, 2001, Representative Turner introduced an identical companion bill to S. 803, H.R. 2458, the E-Government Act of 2001. This bill has been referred to the Committee on Government Reform.

Government Executive magazine reported that in a statement to the Congressional Internet Caucus on March 22, 2001, OMB Deputy Director Sean O'Keefe said that the Bush Administration opposes the creation of a separate federal CIO position in part because of concerns about agency accountability (see [http://www.govexec.com/dailyfed/0301/032301td.htm]). Instead, O'Keefe stated, the Bush Administration intends to recruit a deputy director of management for OMB who will be responsible for oversight of agency-level CIOs and coordinating e-government initiatives.

On June 14, 2001, OMB announced the appointment of Mark Forman to a newly created position, the Associate Director for Information Technology and E-Government.[16] According to the OMB announcement, as "the leading federal e-government executive," the new Associate Director will be responsible for the e-government fund, direct the activities of the CIO Council, and advise on the appointments of agency CIOs. The Associate Director will also "lead the development and implementation of federal information technology policy." The new position will report to the Deputy Director of Management at OMB, who in turn will be the federal CIO.

Provision of Online Services (E-government)[17]

Electronic government (e-government) is an evolving concept, meaning different things to different people. However, it has significant relevance to four important areas of governance: (1) delivery of services (government-to-citizen, or G2C); (2) providing information (also G2C); (3) facilitating the procurement of goods and services (government-to-business, or G2B, and business-to-government, or B2G); and (4) facilitating efficient exchanges within and between agencies (government-to-government, or G2G). For

---

[16] Office of Management and Budget, "Mark Forman Named Associate Director for Information Technology and E-Government," 14 June 2001, [http://www.whitehouse.gov/omb/pubpress/2001-13.html].

[17] See also CRS Report 30745, *Electronic Government: A Conceptual Overview*, by Harold C. Relyea, CRS Report 31088, *Electronic Government: Major Proposals and Initiatives*, by Harold C. Relyea, and CRS Report 31057, *A Primer on E-Government: Sectors, Stages, Opportunities, and Challenges of Online Governance*, by Jeffrey W. Seifert, which are update more frequently than this report.

policymakers concerned about e-government, a central issue is developing a comprehensive but flexible strategy to coordinate the disparate e-government initiatives across the federal government. To that end the Bush Administration proposed a $20 million fund for fiscal 2002, growing to $100 million by the end of fiscal 2004, to support interagency e-government projects. Similarly, Senator Lieberman proposed a $200 million e-government fund in S. 803, the E-Government Act of 2001. Representative Turner also proposed a $200 million fund in H.R. 2458, the E-Government Act of 2001. However, the fiscal 2002 Treasury-Postal Service appropriations bill that was signed into law on November 12, 2001 provided for only $5 million for the e-government fund.

E-government initiatives vary significantly in their breadth and depth from state to state and agency to agency. So far, states such as California, Minnesota, and Utah have taken the lead in developing e-government initiatives. However, there is rapidly increasing interest and activity at the federal level as well. Perhaps the most well-known federal example is the September 2000 launch of the FirstGov web site [http://www.firstgov.gov]. FirstGov is a web portal designed to serve as a single locus point for finding federal government information on the Internet. The FirstGov site also provides access to a variety of state and local government resources. Another example is the Social Security Administration (SSA), which has also launched a number of e-government initiatives including the option to apply for retirement insurance benefits online, request a Social Security Statement, and the ability to request a replacement Medicare card. At the Department of the Treasury, the U.S. Mint is using interactive Internet sales to expand its marketing efforts and attract younger people in coin collecting. Similarly, the General Services Administration (GSA) recently created a new web site, FedBizOpps [http://www.fedbizopps.gov] to facilitate federal business opportunities online. The terrorist attacks of September 11, 2001 and the subsequent anthrax incidents may also motivate new e-government initiatives as Congress considers options to ensure the flow of information and services in the event of future domestic threats.

The movement to put government online raises as many issues as it provides new opportunities. Some of these issues include, but are not limited to: security, privacy, management of governmental technology resources, accessibility of government services (including "digital divide" concerns as a result of a lack of skills or access to computers, discussed earlier), and preservation of public information (maintaining comparable freedom of information procedures for digital documents as exist for paper documents). Although these issues are neither new nor unique to e-government, they do present the challenge of performing governance functions online without sacrificing the accountability of or public access to government that citizens have grown to expect. Some industry groups have also raised concerns about the U.S. government becoming a publicly funded market competitor through the provision of fee-for-services such as the U.S. Postal Service's eBillPay, which allows consumers to schedule and make payments to creditors online [http://www.usps.com/ebpp/welcome.htm].

APPENDIX A: LEGISLATION IN THE 107TH CONGRESS

Following is a topical list of legislation pending before the 107th Congress on the issues covered in this report. The status of the legislation is not provided. For information on legislative status, congressional readers should consult LIS or Thomas, or contact CRS.

Format: Bill Number, Sponsor, Title, Date Introduced, Committee(s) to Which Bill Was Referred

Internet Privacy

H.R. 89, Frelinghuysen, Online Privacy Protection Act, 1/3/01 (Energy & Commerce)

H.R. 91, Frelinghuysen, Social Security Online Privacy Protection Act, 1/3/01 (Energy & Commerce)

H.R. 112, Holt, Electronic Privacy Protection Act, 1/3/01 (Energy & Commerce)

H.R. 220, Paul, Identity Theft Protection Act, 1/3/01 (Ways & Means, Government Reform)

H.R. 237, Eshoo, Consumer Internet Privacy Enhancement Act, 1/20/01 (Energy & Commerce)

H.R. 347, Green, Consumer Online Privacy and Disclosure Act, 1/31/01 (Energy & Commerce)

H.R. 583, Hutchinson, Privacy Commission Act, 2/13/01 (Government Reform)

H.R. 1478, Kleczka, Personal Information Privacy Act, 4/4/01 (Ways & Means, Financial Services)

H.R. 2036, Shaw, Social Security Number Privacy and Identity Theft Prevention Act, 5/25/01 (Ways & Means, Energy & Commerce, Financial Services)

H.R. 2135, Sawyer, Consumer Privacy Protection Act, 6/12/01 (Energy & Commerce)

H.R. 2215, Sensenbrenner, Department of Justice Reauthorization Act, 6/19/01 (Judiciary)

H.R. 3053, Hooley, Identity Theft Protection Act, 10/5/01 (Financial Services)

S. 197, Edwards, Spyware Control and Privacy Protection Act, 1/30/01 (Commerce)
S. 420, Grassley, Bankruptcy Reform Act, 3/1/01 (Judiciary)
S. 803, Lieberman, E-Government Act, 5/1/01 (Government Affairs)
S. 848, Feinstein, Social Security Number Misuse Prevention Act, 5/9/01 (Judiciary)
S. 851, Thompson, Citizen's Privacy Commission Act, 5/9/01 (Governmental Affairs)
S. 1014, Bunning, Social Security Number Privacy and Identity Theft Protection Act, 6/12/01 (Finance)
S. 1055, Feinstein, Privacy Act of 2001, 6/14/01 (Judiciary)
S. 1319, Leahy, Department of Justice Authorization Act, 8/2/01 (Judiciary)
S. 1399, Feinstein, Identity Theft Protection Act, 9/4/01 (Banking)

Computer Security

H.R. 1158, Thornberry, National Homeland Security Agency Act, 3/21/01 (Government Reform)
H.R. 1259, Morella, Computer Security Enhancement Act of 2001, 3/28/01 (Science)
H.R. 1292, Skelton, Homeland Security Strategy Act of 2001, 3/29/01 (Armed Services, Transportation & Infrastructure, Judiciary, Intelligence)
H.R. 2435, Davis, Cyber Security Information Act, 7/10/01 (Government Reform, Judiciary)
H. Con. Res. 22, Saxton, Expressing the sense of Congress regarding Internet security and "cyberterrorism," 2/6/01 (Judiciary, Education & Workforce)

S. 1456, Bennett, Critical Infrastructure Information Security Act of 2001, 9/24/01 (Government Affairs)
S. 1534, Lieberman, Department of National Homeland Security Act of 2001, 10/11/01 (Government Affairs)

Broadband Internet Access

H.R. 267, English, Broadband Internet Access Act of 2001, 1/30/01 (Ways & Means)

H.R. 1415, Rangel, Technology Bond Initiative of 2001, 4/4/01 (Ways & Means)
H.R. 1416, LaFalce, Broadband Expansion Grant Initiative of 2001, 4/4/01 (Energy & Commerce)
H.R. 1542, Tauzin, Internet Freedom and Broadband Deployment Act of 2001, 4/24/01 (Energy & Commerce)
H.R. 1693, R. Hall, Science & Education for the 21st Century Act, 5/3/01 (Science, Education & Workforce)
H.R. 1697, Conyers, Broadband Competition and Incentives Act of 2001, 5/3/01 (Judiciary, Energy & Commerce)
H.R. 1698, Cannon, American Broadband Competition Act of 2001, 5/3/01 (Judiciary, Energy & Commerce)
H.R. 2038, Stupak, Rural Broadband Enhancement Act of 2001, 5/25/01 (Energy & Commerce, Agriculture)
H.R. 2120, Cannon, Broadband Antitrust Restoration and Reform Act, 6/12/01 (Judiciary, Energy & Commerce)
H.R. 2139, Smith, Rural America Digital Accessibility Act, 7/17/01 (Energy & Commerce, Ways & Means, Science)
H.R. 2401, McHugh, Rural America Digital Accessibility Act, 7/17/01 (Energy & Commerce, Ways & Means, Science)
H.R. 2597, McInnis, Broadband Deployment and Telework Incentive Act, 7/23/01 (Ways & Means)
H.R. 2669, Moran, Rural Telecommunications Enhancement Act, 7/27/01 (Agriculture, Energy & Commerce)
H.R. 2847, Boswell, Rural America Technology Enhancement Act, 9/6/01 (Agriculture, Ways & Means, Energy & Commerce, Education & the Workforce)
H.R. 3090, Thomas, Economic Security and Recovery Act, 10/11/01 (H. Ways & Means and S. Finance)

S. 88, Rockefeller, Broadband Internet Access Act of 2001, 1/22/01 (Finance)
S. 150, Kerry, Broadband Deployment Act of 2001, 1/23/01 (Finance)
S. 426, Clinton, Technology Bond Initiative of 2001, 3/1/01 (Finance)
S. 428, Clinton, Broadband Expansion Grant Initiative of 2001, 3/1/01 (Commerce)
S. 430, Clinton, Broadband Rural Research Investment Act of 2001, 3/1/01 (Finance)
S. 966, Dorgan, Rural Broadband Enhancement Act of 2001, 5/25/01 (Commerce)

S. 1126, Brownback, Broadband Deployment and Competition Enhancement Act, 6/28/01 (Commerce)

S. 1127, Brownback, Rural Broadband Deployment Act, 6/28/01 (Commerce)

S. 1571, Lugar, Farm and Ranch Equity Act, 10/18/01 (Agriculture)

S. 1628, Harkin, Agriculture, Conservation, and Rural Enhancement Act, 11/2/01 (Agriculture)

Electronic Commerce

H.R. 89, Frelinghuysen, Online Privacy Protection Act, 1/3/01 (Energy & Commerce)

H.R. 1410, Istook, Internet Tax Simplification Act, 5/9/01 (Judiciary)

H.R. 1552, Cox, Internet Tax Moratorium Act, 5/9/01 (Judiciary)

H.R. 1675, Cox, Permanent Internet Tax Moratorium Act (Judiciary)

S. 288, Wyden, Internet Tax Moratorium Act, 2/8/01 (Commerce, Science & Transportation)

S. 512, Dorgan, Internet Tax Simplification Act, 3/9/01 (Finance)

S. 777, Allen, Permanent Internet Tax Moratorium Act (Commerce, Science & Transportation)

Junk E-Mail

H.R. 95, G. Green, Unsolicited Commercial Electronic Mail Act, 1/3/01 (Energy & Commerce, Judiciary)

H.R. 718, Wilson, Unsolicited Commercial Electronic Mail Act, 2/14/01 (Energy & Commerce, Judiciary)

H.R. 1017, Goodlatte, Anti-Spamming Act, 3/14/01 (Judiciary)

H.R. 3146, C. Smith, Netizens Protection Act, 10/16/01 (Energy & Commerce)

S. 630 (Burns), Can Spam Act, 3/27/01 (Commerce)

Internet Domain Names

H.R. 2417, Shimkus, Dot Kids Domain Name Act, 6/28/01 (Energy & Commerce)

Electronic Government

H.R. 2458, Turner, E-Government Act of 2001, 7/11/01 (Government Reform)

S. 803, Lieberman, E-Government Act of 2001, 5/1/2001 (Government Affairs)

APPENDIX B: LIST OF ACRONYMS

Alphabetically

ACEC	Advisory Commission on Electronic Commerce
B2B	Business-to-Business
B2G	Business-to-Government
BOC	Bell Operating Company
CIO	Chief Information Officer
DMA	Direct Marketing Association
DNS	Domain Name System
DOC	Department of Commerce
EU	European Union
FBI	Federal Bureau of Investigation
FCC	Federal Communications Commission
FTC	Federal Trade Commission
G2B	Government-to-Business
G2C	Government-to-Citizen
G2G	Government-to-Government
GAO	General Accounting Office
GSA	General Services Administration
gTLD	global Top Level Domain
ICANN	Internet Corporation for Assigned Names and Numbers
ILEC	Incumbent Local Exchange Carrier
IP	Internet Protocol
ISP	Internet Service Provider
IT	Information Technology
LATA	Local Access and Transport Area
LEC	Local Exchange Carrier
MOU	Memorandum of Understanding
NGI	Next Generation Internet
NIST	National Institute for Standards and Technology
NSI	Network Solutions, Inc.
NSF	National Science Foundation
NTIA	National Telecommunications and Information Administration
ONDCP	Office of National Drug Control Policy
OPA	Online Privacy Alliance
SSA	Social Security Administration
SSN	Social Security Number

TLD   Top Level Domain
UCE   Unsolicited Commercial E-mail
WIPO   World Intellectual Property Organization
WTO   World Trade Organization

Categorically

U.S. Government Entities

DOC   Department of Commerce
FBI   Federal Bureau of Investigation
FCC   Federal Communications Commission
FTC   Federal Trade Commission
GAO   General Accounting Office
GSA   Government Services Administration
NIST   National Institute of Standards and Technology
        (part of Department of Commerce)
NSF   National Science Foundation
NTIA   National Telecommunications and Information Administration
        (part of Department of Commerce)
ONDCP   Office of National Drug Control Policy
SSA   Social Security Administration

Private Sector Entities

BOC   Bell Operating Company
DMA   Direct Marketing Association
ICANN   Internet Corporation for Assigned Names and Numbers
ILEC   Incumbent Local Exchange Carrier
ISP   Internet Service Provider
LEC   Local Exchange Carrier
NSI   Network Solutions, Inc.
OPA   Online Privacy Alliance

General Types of Internet Services

B2B	Business-to-Business
B2G	Business-to-Government
G2B	Government-to-Business
G2C	Government-to-Citizen
G2G	Government-to-Government

Internet and Telecommunications Terminology

CIO	Chief Information Officer
DNS	Domain Name System
gTLD	global Top Level Domain
IP	Internet Protocol
IT	Information Technology
LATA	Local Access and Transport Area
NGI	Next Generation Internet
TLD	Top Level Domain
UCE	Unsolicited Commercial E-mail

Other

ACEC	Advisory on Electronic Commerce
EU	European Union
MOU	Memorandum of Understanding
SSN	Social Security Number
WIPO	World Intellectual Property Organization
WTO	World Trade Organization

APPENDIX C: LEGISLATION PASSED BY THE 105TH AND 106TH CONGRESSES

Editions of this report prepared in the 105th Congress and the 106th Congress also addressed key technology policy issues affecting the use of growth of the Internet. Some of those issues continue to be of interest to Congress and are discussed in this edition of the report. Others, however, appear to be resolved from a congressional point of view, at least the moment, specifically encryption, electronic signatures, and protecting children from unsuitable material on the Internet. Those topics are not discussed in this version of the report. Nevertheless, it appears useful to retain information about legislation that passed on the subjects of most interest to the two previous Congresses. Following is such a summary, based on the topics that were previously covered in the report.

Legislation Enacted in the 105th Congress

Protecting Children: Child Online Protection Act, Children's Online Privacy Protection Act, and Child Protection and Sexual Predator Protection Act

In the FY1999 Omnibus Consolidated and Emergency Supplemental Appropriations Act (P.L. 105-277), Congress included several provisions related to protecting children on the Internet. Included is legislation making it a crime to send material that is "harmful to minors" to children and protecting the privacy of information provided by children under 13 over interactive computer services. Separately, Congress passed a law (P.L. 105-314) that, *inter alia*, strengthens penalties against sexual predators using the Internet.

The "harmful to minors" language is in the **Child Online Protection Act**, Title XIV of Division C of the Omnibus Appropriations Act. Similar language was also included in the Internet Tax Freedom Act (Title XI of Division C of the Omnibus Appropriations Act). Called "CDA II" by some in reference to the Communications Decency Act that passed Congress in 1996 but was overturned by the Supreme court, the bill restricts access to commercial material that is "harmful to minors" distributed on the World Wide Web to those 17 and older. The American Civil Liberties Union (ACLU) and others filed suit against enforcement of the portion of the Act dealing with the "harmful to minors" language. In February 1999, a federal judge in Philadelphia issued a preliminary injunction against enforcement of that section of the Act. The Justice Department has filed an appeal.

The **Children's Online Privacy Protection Act**, also part of the Omnibus Appropriations Act (Title XIII of Division C), requires verifiable parental consent for the collection, use, or dissemination of personally identifiable information from children under 13.

The Omnibus Appropriation Act also includes a provision intended to make it easier for the FBI to gain access to Internet service provider records of suspected sexual predators (Section 102, General Provisions, Justice Department). It also sets aside $2.4 million for the Customs Service to double the staffing and resources for the child pornography cyber-smuggling initiative and provides $1 million in the Violent Crime Reduction Trust Fund for technology support for that initiative.

The **Protection of Children from Sexual Predators Act** (P.L. 105-314) is a broad law addressing concerns about sexual predators. Among its provisions are increased penalties for anyone who uses a computer to persuade, entice, coerce, or facilitate the transport of a child to engage in prohibited sexual activity, a requirement that Internet service providers report to law enforcement if they become aware of child pornography activities, a requirement that federal prisoners using the Internet be supervised, and a requirement for a study by the National Academy of Sciences on how to reduce the availability to children of pornography on the Internet.

Identity Theft and Assumption Deterrence Act

The Identity Theft and Assumption Deterrence Act (P.L. 105-318) sets penalties for persons who knowingly, and with the intent to commit unlawful activities, possess, transfer, or use one or more means of identification not legally issued for use to that person.

Intellectual Property: Digital Millennium Copyright Act

Congress passed legislation (P.L. 105-304) implementing the World Intellectual Property Organization (WIPO) treaties regarding protection of copyright on the Internet. The law also limits copyright infringement liability for online service providers that serve only as conduits of information. Provisions relating to database protection that were included by the House were not included in the enacted version and are being debated anew in the

106th Congress. Since database protection per se is not an Internet issue, it is not included in this report.

Digital Signatures: Government Paperwork Elimination Act

Congress passed the Government Paperwork Elimination Act (Title XVII of Division C of the Omnibus Appropriations Act, P.L. 105-277) that directs the Office of Management and Budget to develop procedures for the use and acceptance of "electronic" signatures (of which digital signatures are one type) by executive branch agencies.

Internet Domain Names: Next Generation Internet Research Act

The Next Generation Internet Research Act (P.L. 105-305) directs the National Academy of Sciences to conduct a study of the short and long-term effects on trademark rights of adding new generation top-level domains and related dispute resolution procedures.

Summary of Legislation Passed by the 105th Congress

Title	Public Law Number
FY1999 Omnibus Consolidated and Emergency Supplemental Appropriations Act	P.L. 105-277
Internet Tax Freedom Act	Division C, Title XI
Children's Online Privacy Protection Act	Division C, Title XIII
Child Online Protection Act	Division C, Title XIV
Government Paperwork Elimination Act	Division C, Title XVII
Protection of Children from Sexual Predators Act	P.L. 105-314
Identity Theft and Assumption Deference Act	P.L. 105-318
Digital Millennium Copyright Act	P.L. 105-304
Next Generation Internet Research Act	P.L. 105-305

Legislation Enacted in the 106th Congress

Electronic Signatures

The **Millennium Digital Commerce Act (P.L. 106-229)** regulates Internet electronic commerce by permitting and encouraging its continued expansion through the operation of free market forces, including the legal recognition of electronic signatures and electronic records.

Computer Security

The **Computer Crime Enforcement Act (P.L. 106-572)** establishes Department of Justice grants to state and local authorities to help them investigate and prosecute computer crimes. The law authorizes the expenditure of $25 million for the grant program through FY2004. The **FY2001 Department of Defense Authorization Act (P.L. 106-398)** includes language that originated in S. 1993 to modify the Paperwork Reduction Act and other relevant statutes concerning computer security of government systems, codifying agency responsibilities regarding computer security.

Internet Privacy

Language in the **FY2001 Transportation Appropriations Act (P.L. 106-246)** and the **FY2001 Treasury-General Government Appropriations Act** (included as part of the Consolidated Appropriations Act, P.L. 106-554) addresses Web site information collection practices by departments and agencies in the Treasury-General Government Appropriations Act. Section 501 of the FY2001 Transportation Appropriations Act prohibits funds in the FY2001 Treasury-General Government Appropriations Act from being used by any federal agency to collect, review, or create aggregate lists that include personally identifiable information (PII) about an individual's access to or use of a federal Web site, or enter into agreements with third parties to do so, with exceptions. Section 646 of the FY2001 Treasury-General Government Appropriations Act requires Inspectors General of agencies or departments covered in that act to report to Congress within 60 days of enactment on activities by those agencies or departments relating to the collection of PII about individuals who access any Internet site of that department or agency, or entering into agreements with third parties to obtain PII about use of government or non-government Web sites.

The **Social Security Number Confidentiality Act (P.L. 106-433)** prohibits the display of Social Security numbers on unopened checks or other Treasury-issued drafts. (Although this is not an Internet issue, it is related to concerns about consumer identity theft, a topic addressed in this report.)

The **Internet False Identification Prevention Act (P.L. 106-578)** updates existing law against selling or distributing false identification documents to include those sold or distributed through computer files, templates, and disks. It also requires the Attorney General and Secretary of the Treasury to create a coordinating committee to ensure that the creation and distribution of false Ids is vigorously investigated and prosecuted.

Protecting Children from Unsuitable Material

The Children's Internet Protection Act (Title XVII of the FY2001 Labor-HHS Appropriations Act, included in the FY2001 Consolidated Appropriations Act, P.L. 106-554) requires most schools and libraries that receive federal funding through Title III of the Elementary and Secondary Education Act, the Museum and Library Services Act, or "E-rate" subsidies from the universal service fund, to use technology protection measures (filtering software or other technologies) to block certain Web sites when computers are being used by minors, and in some cases, by adults. When minors are using the computers, the technology protection measure must block access to visual depictions that are obscene, child pornography, or harmful to minors. When others are using the computers, the technology must block visual depictions that are obscene or are child pornography. The technology protection measure may be disabled by authorized persons to enable access for bona fide research or other lawful purposes.

Internet Domain Names

The **Anticybersquatting Consumer Protection Act (part of the FY2000 Consolidated Appropriations Act, P.L. 106-113)** gives courts the authority to order the forfeiture, cancellation, and/or transfer of domain names registered in "bad faith" that are identical or similar to trademarks. The Act provides for statutory civil damages of at least $1,000, but not more than $100,000 per domain name identifier.

Summary of Legislation Enacted in the 106th Congress

Title	Public Law Number
Millennium Digital Commerce Act	P.L. 106-229
Computer Crime Enforcement Act	P.L. 106-572
FY2001 Transportation Appropriations Act, section 501	P.L. 106-246
FY2001 Treasury-General Government Appropriations Act, section 646 (enacted by reference in the FY2001 Consolidated Appropriations Act)	P.L. 106-554
Social Security Number Confidentiality Act	P.L. 106-433
Internet False Identification Prevention Act	P.L. 106-578
Children's Internet Protection Act (Title XVII of the FY2001 Labor-HHS Appropriations Act, enacted by reference in the FY2001 Consolidated Appropriations Act)	P.L. 106-554
Anticybersquatting Consumer Protection Act (enacted by reference in the FY2000 Consolidated Appropriations Act)	P.L. 106-113

INDEX

A

advertising, 20, 25, 26
Advisory Commission on Electronic Commerce (ACEC), 23, 44, 46
American Civil Liberties Union (ACLU), 7, 47
anti-drug campaign, 4
AOL, 18
At-Large Membership Study Committee (ALSC), 30

B

banking, 10, 12
Bell Atlantic, 15
Bell Operating Company (BOC), 15, 16, 44, 45
Better Business Bureau, 3
Broadband Internet Access, 14, 18, 40, 41
broadband, vii, 14, 15, 17, 18
Bureau of Export Administration, 22
Bush Administration, 10, 13, 21, 36, 37
Bush, President, 24

C

Center for Democracy and Technology (CDT), 7
Chief Information Officer (CIO), 34-36, 44, 46
Child Online Protection Act, 47, 49
Children's Internet Protection Act, 51, 52
Children's Online Privacy Protection Act (COPPA), 3, 47-49
Clinton Administration, 2, 21, 22, 27, 32
Clinton, President, 4, 10, 23, 32
Coalition Against Commercial Email (CAUCE), 25
Code Red II, 9
Code Red, 9, 10
Commercial Electronic Mail, 25, 42
Commercial Web Sites, 2
Communications Decency Act, 47
Computer Emergency Response Team (CERT), 9, 12
Computer Security Act, 11, 13
computer security, vii, 9, 11, 13, 40, 50
Consolidated Appropriations Act, 2, 4, 31, 50-52
Consumer Identity Theft, 8

Consumer Internet Privacy
 Enhancement Act, 39
credit card numbers, 2, 10
credit card, 2, 8
criminals, 9, 11

D

Department of Commerce (DOC), 4,
 19, 22, 27-29, 44, 45
Department of Defense Advanced
 Research Projects Agency
 (DARPA), 27
Department of Defense Authorization
 Act, 50
Department of the Treasury, 37
Digital Millennium Copyright Act,
 48, 49
Digital Signatures, 49
digital subscriber line (DSL), 14, 17
Direct Marketing Association
 (DMA), 26, 44, 45
Domain Name System (DNS), vii,
 27-30, 44, 46

E

e-commerce security, 22, 24
e-commerce taxation, 23
e-commerce, vii, 19-24
e-government, vii, 32, 34, 36, 37
electronic commerce, vii, 19, 21, 24,
 42, 46, 49
electronic government, 36
Electronic Privacy Information
 Center (EPIC), 7
electronic signatures, 22
Employer Monitoring, 7
European Union (EU), 22, 24, 44, 46
export policy, 22

F

fair information practices, 2, 3

Federal Bureau of Investigation
 (FBI), 5, 9, 10, 12, 44, 45, 48
Federal Communications
 Commission (FCC), 14, 17, 18,
 44, 45
Federal Information Security Reform
 Act, 12, 13
Federal Trade Commission (FTC), 2,
 3, 8, 18, 25, 44, 45
Federal Web Sites, 3
finance, 10, 12
Freedom of Information Act (FOIA),
 14

G

General Accounting Office (GAO),
 5, 11, 12, 35, 44, 45
General Services Administration
 (GSA), 37, 44, 45
generic Top Level Domains (gTLDs),
 27, 28
global electronic signatures, 23
gross domestic product (GDP), 20, 21

H

Homeland Security Strategy Act, 13,
 40

I

ICANN, 27-31, 44, 45
Identity Theft and Assumption
 Deterrence Act, 8, 48
Identity Theft, 8, 39, 40, 48, 49
Information Sharing and Analysis
 Centers (ISACs), 12
Information Technology (IT), 13, 32,
 33, 35, 36, 44, 46
Inspectors General (IGs), 4, 5, 50
interLATA, 16

Index

International Common Criteria for Information Technology Security Evaluation, 13
International Data Corporation (IDC), 12, 19
Internet activity, 1, 6
Internet Corporation for Assigned Names and Numbers, 27, 44, 45
Internet Domain Names, v, 27, 43, 49, 51
Internet False Identification Act, 8
Internet False Identification Prevention Act, 51, 52
Internet Privacy, 1, 2, 5, 13, 39, 50
Internet Protocol (IP), 27, 28, 30, 44, 46
Internet Service Provider (ISP), 5, 6, 15, 17, 18, 25, 26, 44, 45
Internet Tax Freedom Act, 23, 47, 49
Internet Tax Nondiscrimination Act, 23

J

junk e-mail, vii, 25, 26, 42
Justice Department, 6, 48

L

Local Exchange Carrier (LEC), 44, 45
Love Bug virus, 10

M

Memorandum of Understanding (MOU), 27, 28, 44, 46

N

National Homeland Security Agency, 14, 40
National Institute of Standards and Technology (NIST), 11, 13, 44, 45
National Policy, 32
National Science Foundation (NSF), 27, 33, 44, 45
National Security Agency, 11
Networking and Information Technology Research Development Act, 33
Next Generation Internet (NGI), 33, 44, 46, 49
Notice of Inquiry (NOI), 18

O

Office of Management and Budget (OMB), 4, 5, 11-13, 34-36, 49
Office of National Drug Control Policy (ONDCP), 4, 44, 45
Online Privacy Alliance (OPA), 3, 44, 45

P

Partnership for Critical Infrastructure Security, 12
personal information, 2, 4, 5, 8
Presidential Decision Directive (PDD), 10, 12
Privacy Act, 4, 39, 40
Privacy Protection Act, 39, 40, 42
private sector, vii, 1, 10, 14, 20, 27, 29, 34

R

Research & Development, 33

S

satellite broadband, 17
self regulation, 2, 3
September 11th, 1, 6, 11, 21, 22, 30, 37
sexual predators, 47, 48

Social Security Administration (SSA), 37, 44, 45
Social Security Number (SSN), 8, 39, 40, 44, 46, 50, 52
Social Security Number Confidentiality Act, 8, 50, 52
Social Security numbers, 2, 8, 50
spam, vii, 25, 26
spyware, 7, 8, 40

T

Telecommunications Act, 14-16
Telephone Consumer Protection Act, 25
terrorism, 1, 6, 11
Time Warner, 18
Top Level Domain (TLD), 28, 29, 44-46
Transportation Appropriations Act, 2, 4, 50, 52
transportation systems, 10
Treasury-General Government Appropriations Act, 4, 50, 52
Treasury-Postal Appropriations Act, 4, 5
TRUSTe, 3

U

unauthorized use, 2, 9, 10
uniform dispute resolution policy (UDRP), 31
unsolicited commercial electronic mail (UCE), vii, 25, 26, 45, 46
USA PATRIOT Act, 6, 22

V

Verizon, 15

W

Web Site Operators, 2
WebTrust, 3
White House, 4, 34, 35
World Intellectual Property Organization (WIPO), 31, 45, 46, 48
World Trade Organization (WTO), 21, 22, 24, 45, 46